# Counted Cross-Stitch Patterns and Designs

Compiled by
**The Swedish Handcraft Society**

*Translated from the Swedish
by Alice Blomquist*

BELL & HYMAN

LONDON

First published in Great Britain in 1981
by Bell & Hyman Limited
  Denmark House
  37-39 Queen Elizabeth Street
  London SE1 2QB

Copyright © 1976 Föreningen Svensk Hemslöjd
English translation © 1981 Charles Scribner's Sons

Original Swedish edition published by Lts förlag, Stockholm
Translated by Alice Blomquist

**British Library Cataloguing in Publication Data**

Counted cross-stitch patterns and designs.
  1. Cross-stitch—Sweden—Patterns
  I. Swedish Handcraft Society
  II. Korsstygns boken. English
  746.44′041    TT778.C76

  ISBN 0-7135-1276-8

Printed in the United States

# Contents

# Foreword

Even those people who have little training in embroidery can sew cross stitch, which is an easy technique. This is probably one of the reasons cross-stitch embroidery is so popular, now that so many people are working outside the home and have less time for leisure activities.

Long-legged cross stitch has been cherished for centuries in Sweden, especially in the province of Skåne. The technique can even be used in modern work and with nontraditional materials, and we have chosen some patterns where it is used in an unusual way.

If the details of the patterns inspire embroidery in other color and pattern combinations than have been suggested here, then we have achieved our goal with this book. It is our sincere wish that it be a source of delight and inspiration to all who look for new patterns.

And our warm thanks to all who have contributed to this book.

Stig-Thore Nilsson and the
Swedish Handcraft Society

# Cross Stitch and Long-legged Cross Stitch

Cross stitch and long-legged cross stitch (the latter known as *tvistsöm* in Sweden) are both very old decorative stitches that are seen throughout Sweden in peasant embroidery and in embroidery for the nobility. Cross-stitch embroidery has been popular since the sixteenth century, when it was widely used on a variety of items. The designs were taken mainly from German and Italian pattern books, which could be found all over Europe at that time.

Embroidery in red on a white background was particularly common in the Swedish provinces of Gästrikland, Hälsingland, and Dalarna. These provinces have magnificent cross-stitch embroidery on linen.

During the nineteenth century, particularly, cross stitch was embroidered on articles of clothing as well as on most household textiles. Sometimes cross stitch was combined with other stitches or sewn on a

Hanging drapery from the end of the nineteenth century. White cotton cloth with cross-stitch border embroidered with red cotton yarn. *Photo courtesy of Nordiska Museum, Stockholm*

Splendid travel cushion from Skåne in long-legged cross stitch, with pomegranate pattern. Signed "KLD, 1775." 156 × 56 cm. (61.5 × 22 in.). *Photo courtesy of Carl Meijer*

piece of fabric that was later sewn into another kind of work. Bed linens, bridegrooms' shirts, and other textiles were signed with the very finest cross stitches and often edged with flowers, hearts, or crown designs.

Samplers have been stitched in Sweden since the eighteenth century and have been very important in keeping the traditional patterns alive (see "Johanna's Sampler" on page 40). These samplers show examples of suitable designs in cross stitch and include numbers and the alphabet as well.

Long-legged cross stitch is much like regular cross stitch, except that one of the stitches is twice as long as the other. It was originally sewn on a coarse tabby weave and, later, even on canvas.

An abundant amount of embroidery in long-legged cross stitch is found in the province of Skåne. In many homes there are antique heirloom cushions or pillows in magnificent colors. Patterns are usually taken from the sixteenth and seventeenth centuries, when long-legged cross stitch was most often used. Usually there are repeated patterns that cover the whole surface in squares or in zigzag or star forms. Typical motifs for the long-legged cross stitch from Skåne are oak leaves, tulips, pomegranates, and palmettes. The borders usually have figure-eights or stylized leaf designs.

# Technique

Cross stitch should always be sewn on a material where the threads can be counted. Unless otherwise stated in the pattern instructions, you should sew over 2 × 2 threads in the weave. On Linneaida, however, a stitch is made over each thread cross.

The understitches are first sewn from left to right (Figure 1), then the overstitches are sewn from right to left (Figure 2). The overstitches in a cross-stitch embroidery pattern should always lie in the same direction. Therefore, depending on the form of the pattern, one must sometimes sew cross stitch in vertical rows (Figures 3 and 4).

On the back side of the embroidery there should be only vertical stitches. Fastening of the threads on the back side is done by drawing the threads under the stitches in the direction of the stitches.

2

1

3

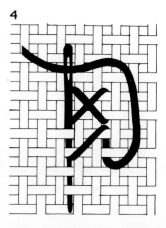

4

**Long-legged cross stitch** is also sewn over counted threads in linen. The stitch is much like regular cross stitch; the difference is that one alternately sews short stitches (over 2 threads) and long stitches (over 4 threads), giving the work a braidlike effect.

Figure 1 shows how the first row is sewn. Begin with a short stitch from left to right *(a)*. Continue with a short stitch from right to left *(b),* and then a long stitch from left to right *(c)*. Then continue with one short, one long, one short, and so on. The row ends with a short stitch.

Figure 2 shows the first row as before, sewn from left to right, and how the second row is sewn back from right to left without turning the work. The third row is sewn as the first, the fourth as the second, and so forth. This is called one-row long-legged cross stitch.

In Figure 3 the first row (the lower row in the diagram) was sewn as in Figure 1, from left to right. The embroidery was then turned upside down so that the second row (the top row in Figure 3) could also be sewn from left to right. After a new turn, the third row is sewn as the first, and so forth. One turns the work for each row and can therefore sew from left to right the entire time. This is called two-row long-legged cross stitch. It gives a more wide-striped appearance than the one-row stitch. Notice the difference in how the long stitches lie in Figures 2 and 3.

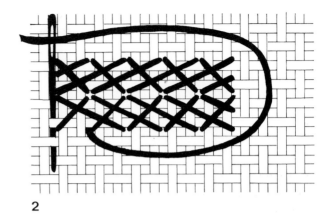

2

3

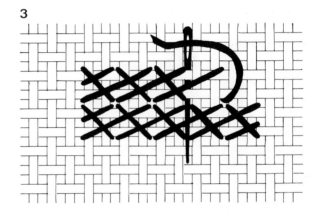

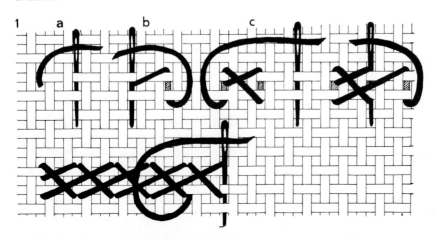

1     a         b         c

On long-legged cross-stitch patterns there are often arrows for each section that show in which direction the rows of stitches should be sewn. If no direction is marked on the pattern, one should usually sew lengthways on each section. The yarn should completely cover the surface, so the stitches must not be drawn too firmly. For this reason, long-legged cross stitch should preferably be sewn in an embroidery frame (see page 70).

Fastening of the yarn is done on the front side of the embroidery by drawing the threads under the sewn stitches in the direction of the row.

**Backstitch** is often used in combination with cross stitch when contours and outlines are to be sewn (see diagram below).

# Materials

The following are lists of embroidery yarns and linen fabrics that have been used for the patterns in this book.

## Yarns

KL = Klippans linen yarn 16/2
N  = Niabs linen yarn 16/2
HF = Haandarbejdets Fremmes cotton yarn 24/2
HV = Handarbetets Vänners linen yarn 40/2
B  = Bergå tapestry wool 5.5/2

These yarns may be ordered directly from the Swedish Handcraft Society: Föreningen Svensk Hemslöjd, Sveavägen 44, 111 34 Stockholm, Sweden. HF cotton yarn may be purchased in the United States and Great Britain; see the list of suppliers on page 71. The colors have also been converted as closely as possible to DMC (demercerized cotton) color numbers, which have been given in each pattern. In some instances the color comparisons are not good and in others there is no color comparison; this has been noted in the patterns.

The suggestions below show suitable yarn for the respective linens.

### For cross-stitch embroidery

| | | |
|---|---|---|
| Bohuslinne | 14 threads/cm. (35.5/in.) | HF cotton yarn 24/2 |
| Fyenlinne | 13 threads/cm. (33/in.) | HF cotton yarn 24/2 |
| D-linne | 12 threads/cm. (30.5/in.) | HF cotton yarn 24/2 |
| D-linne | 10 threads/cm. (25.5/in.) | HF cotton yarn 24/2 |
| Irlandialinne II | 10 threads/cm. (25.5/in.) | HV linen yarn 40/2 |
| Skolline II | 10.5 threads/cm. (26.5/in.) | Linen yarn 16/2 or HV linen yarn 40/2 |
| Skånelinne | 9 threads/cm. (23/in.) | Linen yarn 16/2 |
| Dalalinne | 7.5 threads/cm. (19/in.) | Linen yarn 16/2 |
| Dalalinne | 7.5 threads/cm. (19/in.) | HF cotton yarn 24/2 (2 threads) |
| Linneaida | 3.5 stitches/cm. (9/in.) | Bergå tapestry wool 5.5/2 |

*For long-legged cross-stitch embroidery*

| | | |
|---|---|---|
| Irlandialinne II | 10 threads/cm. (25.5/in.) | HF cotton yarn 24/2 (2 threads) |
| Irlandialinne II | 10 threads/cm. (25.5/in.) | HV linen yarn 40/2 (2 threads) |
| Dalalinne | 7.5 threads/cm. (19/in.) | Linen yarn 16/2 |
| Dalalinne | 7.5 threads/cm. (19/in.) | HF cotton yarn 24/2 (3 threads) |
| Dalalinne | 7.5 threads/cm. (19/in.) | HV linen yarn 40/2 (3 threads) |
| Linneaida | 3.5 stitches/cm. (9/in.) | Bergå tapestry wool 5.5/2 |

These linen fabrics may be ordered directly from the Swedish Handcraft Society, or comparable linens may be obtained from needlecraft stores in the United States and Great Britain. See page 71 for a list of some of the suppliers of imported yarns and linens. It should be noted that linen with the same number of threads per inch may have different names when it comes from different manufacturers.

The thickness of the yarn must be well suited to the fabric it is sewn on, or the embroidery will not look right. Many of the patterns may be sewn on coarser linen with thicker yarns, with good results, even if finer qualities have been used here. Most of the embroidery sewn with one-thread cotton yarn on a fabric with 30 or 33 threads to the inch may be sewn with two threads of the same yarn on a fabric with 23 or 19 threads to the inch.

If the embroidery is to be done on a different material from that given in the pattern, one can easily calculate how large the work will be according to the following:

$$\frac{\text{Piece's finished measurements} \times \text{number of threads/in. in the linen}}{\text{Number of threads/in. in the linen one will sew on}}$$

For example:

One wants to sew a cloth on linen with 26.5 threads/in. using a pattern with the given finished size 12 × 12 inches, on Fyenlinne with 33 threads/in. Therefore,

$$\frac{12 \times 33}{26.5} = \frac{396}{26.5} = 14.94 \text{ inches}$$

The cloth will be 15 × 15 inches on the new linen. Allowances for hems must be added to this measurement.

# Cross-Stitch Patterns

# "TOWN SQUARE"
## (wall hanging)

**Pattern by:** Anette Eriksson
**Cut Size:** 30 × 30 cm. (12 × 12 in.)
**Finished Size:** 21.5 × 21.5 cm. (8.5 × 8.5 in.)
**Technique:** Cross stitch
**Materials:** D-linne, 10 threads/cm. (25.5 threads/in.); HF cotton yarn

Follow the arrows on the graph and find the middle. Begin the embroidery in the middle of the linen.

## Yarn colors (DMC)

| | | | |
|---|---|---|---|
| HF no. 22 (322) | | HF no. 229 (932) | |
| HF no. 303 (415) | | HF no. 25 (950) | |
| HF no. 216 (3031) | | HF no. 231 (503) | |
| HF no. 95 (921) | | HF no. 218 (613) | |
| HF no. 28 (677) | | HF no. 54 (782) | |
| HF no. 213 (780) | | | |

The word *Stortorget*, Swedish for "town square," is sewn in backstitch in HF no. 216 (3031).

### Finishing

See directions for the "Living Room" pattern on page 21.

STORTORGET

"*Stortorget*" is a design taken from the southwest side of the town square in Stockholm's Old Town and is easily recognized by both natives and visitors who have wandered over the cobblestones there. If you wish to make the picture larger, use double yarn on Dalalinne.

# "KITCHEN," "DINING ROOM," and "LIVING ROOM"
## (wall hangings)

### "Kitchen"

**Pattern by:** Margareta Harström
**Cut Size:** 25 × 30 cm. (10 × 12 in.)
**Finished Size:** 18.5 × 25 cm. (7¼ × 10 in.)
**Technique:** Cross stitch
**Materials:** D-linne, 12 threads/cm. (30.5 threads/in.); HF cotton yarn

Measure 2.5 cm. (1 in.) in from the edge of the linen, from above and from the left, and begin the embroidery at the arrow.

**Yarn colors (DMC)**

| | | | | |
|---|---|---|---|---|
| HF no. 216 (3031) | ▬ | HF no. 240 (310) | ╫ | |
| HF no. 17 (797) | ••• | HF no. 213 (780) | sss | |
| | | HF no. 19 (452) | ╫╫ | |

**Finishing**
See page 21.

"Kitchen," "Dining Room," and "Living Room" are three small wall hangings that may also be embroidered in a row on one piece of fabric. They give the impression of old-fashioned coziness. Certainly one can hear the clock ticking in the kitchen or the cat purring on the chair in the dining room, and feel the Sunday peacefulness surrounding the sofa in the living room.

Linen may vary somewhat in the number of threads per inch, so it is best to buy linen for all the hangings at once. Also, the embroidery must be done in the same direction on all three pieces; otherwise they may turn out to be of different sizes.

### "Dining Room"

**Pattern by:** Margareta Harström
**Cut Size:** 25 × 30 cm. (10 × 12 in.)
**Finished Size:** 18.5 × 25 cm. (7¼ × 10 in.)
**Technique:** Cross stitch
**Materials:** D-linne, 12 threads/cm. (30.5 threads/in.); HF cotton yarn

Measure 2.5 cm. (1 in.) in from the edge of the linen, from above and from the left, and begin the embroidery at the arrow.

**Yarn colors (DMC)**

| | | | |
|---|---|---|---|
| HF no. 216 (3031) | ▬ | HF no. 240 (310) | ⊞ |
| HF no. 17 (797) | ••• | HF no. 95 (921) | ××× |
| HF no. 2 (899) | ⋁⋁⋁ | HF no. 54 (782) | ⁄⁄⁄ |
| | | HF no. 10 (320) | ∘∘∘ |

**Finishing**
See page 21.

# "Living Room"

**Pattern by:** Margareta Harström
**Cut Size:** 25 × 30 cm. (10 × 12 in.)
**Finished Size:** 18.5 × 25 cm. (7¼ × 10 in.)
**Technique:** Cross stitch
**Materials:** D-linne, 12 threads/cm. (30.5 threads/in.); HF cotton yarn

Measure 2.5 cm. (1 in.) in from the edge of the linen, from above and from the left, and begin the embroidery at the arrow.

**Yarn colors (DMC)**

| | | | |
|---|---|---|---|
| HF no. 216 (3031) | | HF no. 95 (921) | |
| HF no. 17 (797) | | HF no. 54 (782) | |
| HF no. 2 (899) | | HF no. 10 (320) | |
| HF no. 213 (780) | | HF no. 25 (950) | |

20

### Finishing

Cut a firm piece of cardboard the size of the finished wall hanging. Fold the embroidery over the edges and cover with a backing of the same linen fabric, sewn in place with slip stitch. Attach two small metal rings at the upper corners on the back of the hanging and fasten a string between the rings.

# "CLOVER" and "WHITE WOOD ANEMONE"
## (place mats and plate liners)

### "Clover"

*Pattern by:* Kristina Domellöf
*Technique:* Cross stitch
*Materials:* Fyenlinne, 13 threads/cm. (33 threads/in.); HF cotton yarn

### Place mat

*Cut Size:* 40 × 50 cm. (16 × 20 in.)
*Finished Size:* 32 × 43 cm. (12½ × 17 in.)

Follow the arrows on the pattern to the middle. Measure 10 cm. (4 in.) from above and 10 cm. (4 in.) from the left short side of the linen. This point is the same as the middle point of the pattern; begin the embroidery there. The hem is made 8 threads wide in plain hemstitch (see page 68). The distance from the hem to the pattern is 10 threads.

### Plate liner

*Cut Size:* 20 × 20 cm. (8 × 8 in.)
*Finished Size:* 15 × 15 cm. (6 × 6 in.)

Follow the arrows on the pattern to the middle, and begin the embroidery there. The hem is folded 7.5 cm. (3 in.) from the middle of the embroidery, and should be made 8 threads wide in plain hemstitch.

### Yarn colors (DMC)

HF no. 205 (600)
HF no.   3 (3688)
HF no. 231 (503)
HF no. 100 (367)
HF no.   8 (992/not good)

**Januari**
*V1*

**1**

**Torsdag"**

Nyårsdagen

Place mats and plate liners with small flower designs are very popular handwork. The flowers may also be used as decoration on other pieces, such as the embroidered wall calendar shown here.

### "White Wood Anemone"

*Pattern by:* Kristina Domellöf
*Size:* See measurements for "Clover" place mat and plate liner on page 22.
*Technique:* Cross stitch and backstitch
*Materials:* Fyenlinne, 13 threads/cm. (33 threads/in.); HF cotton yarn and HV linen yarn no. 40/2

*Yarn colors (DMC)*

Cross stitch HF no. 3 (3688)

Cross stitch HF no. 8 (992/not good)

Cross stitch HF no. 47 (734)

Cross stitch HV no. 1 (blanc)

Cross stitch HF no. 10 (320)

Backstitch HV no. 1 (blanc)

# "MIDSUMMER RING"
## (table runner)

*Pattern by:* Stig-Thore Nilsson
*Cut Size:* 25 × 100 cm. (10 × 39⅜ in.)
*Finished Size:* 15.5 × 90.5 cm. (6 × 35⅝ in.)
*Technique:* Cross stitch and backstitch
*Materials:* D-linne, 12 threads/cm. (30.5 threads/in.); HF cotton yarn

Measure 6 cm. (2⅓ in.) in from the edge in the middle of the short side of the linen. Begin the embroidery at the arrow. The complete table runner is seven rings in length. Notice the change of color in every other ring. The hem is folded 36 threads outside the pattern and is 8 threads wide.

### Yarn colors (DMC)

| | |
|---|---|
| Cross stitch HF no. 17 (797) | ▬ |
| Cross stitch HF no. 506 (3347/not good) | ••• |
| Cross stitch HF no. 22 (322) | ∕∕∕ |
| Cross stitch HF no. 53 (977) | ᴡᴡᴡ |
| Cross stitch HF no. 504 (900) | ×××  |
| Cross stitch HF no. 100 (367) | ₀₀₀ |
| Backstitch HF no. 504 (900) | |
| Backstitch HF no. 22 (322) | ◿ |

The "Midsummer Ring" table runner is formed of the rings from the midsummer pole in the "Midsummer Dance" pattern on page 41. If one prefers a larger tablecloth, one may place the rings in a row in the middle of the cloth, as on the table runner, or in a circle, if the cloth is to be used on a round table. The design may be sewn with the same yarn on D-linne if one wishes the embroidery to be somewhat larger.

The small flowers from the midsummer pole may easily be recognized here on the small cloth "Summer Flowers," though the colors are different. This cloth may be made larger if one uses thicker yarn on a coarser linen. One could also make a place mat with a row of flowers on one side. (See page 26 for instructions for "Summer Flowers.")

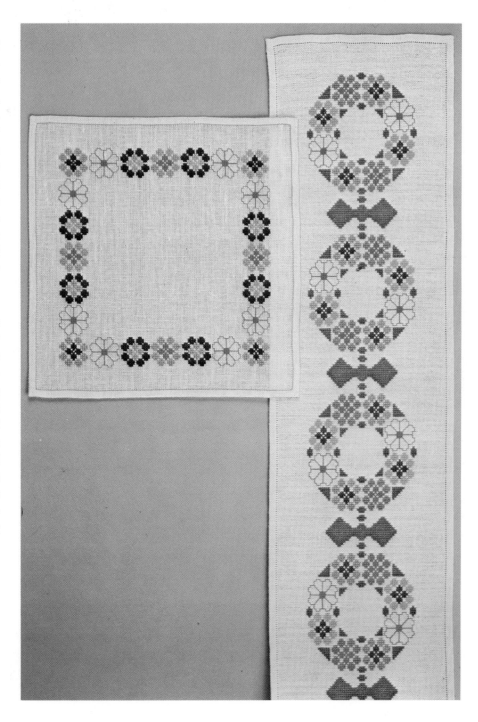

# "SUMMER FLOWERS"
## (cloth)

*Pattern by:* Stig-Thore Nilsson
*Cut Size:* 30 × 30 cm. (12 × 12 in.)
*Finished Size:* 22 × 22 cm. (8⅔ × 8⅔ in.)
*Technique:* Cross stitch and backstitch
*Materials:* Fyenlinne, 13 threads/cm. (33 threads/in.); HF cotton yarn

The arrow on the pattern indicates the starting point, the middle of the side of the cloth.

The hem is folded at the outermost backstitch row and is hemmed at the inside row.

*Yarn colors (DMC)*
Cross stitch HF no. 220 (336)
Cross stitch HF no. 506
(3347/not good)
Cross stitch HF no. 504 (900)
Backstitch HF no. 506
(3347/not good)
Backstitch HF no.  22 (322)
Backstitch HF no. 504 (900)

See color plate on page 25.

# "ROCKROSE"
## (cloth)

*Pattern by:* Stig-Thore Nilsson
*Cut Size:* 30 × 30 cm. (12 × 12 in.)
*Finished Size:* 24 × 24 cm. (9½ × 9½ in.)
*Technique:* Cross stitch
*Materials:* Fyenlinne, 13 threads/cm. (33 threads/in.); HF cotton yarn

The arrow indicates the middle of the side of the cloth. The hem folds at the outermost cross-stitch row and is hemmed in the fourth row.

*Yarn colors (DMC)*
HF no. 508 (911) o o o
HF no. 505 (704) ×××
HF no. 210 (500) ▬
HF no.  54 (782) • • •
HF no.  26 (733) ⧺⧺⧺

See color plate on page 29.

27

# "AUGUST VINE"
## (cloth)

**Pattern by:** Stig-Thore Nilsson
**Cut Size:** 35 × 35 cm. (13¾ × 13¾ in.)
**Finished Size:** 29 × 29 cm. (11⅜ × 11⅜ in.)
**Technique:** Cross stitch
**Materials:** Fyenlinne, 13 threads/cm. (33 threads/in.); HF cotton yarn

The hem is folded 13 threads outside the pattern and is 8 threads wide. The arrow indicates the middle of the side of the cloth.

### Yarn colors (DMC)

HF no. 206 (3051)
HF no.  26 (733)
HF no. 101 (988)
HF no. 505 (704)

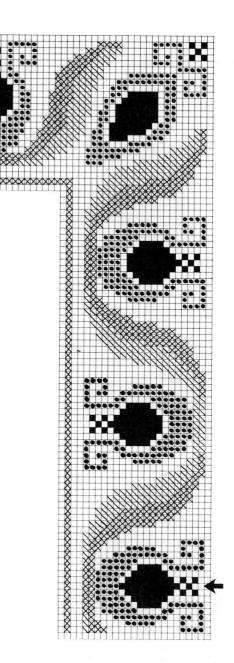

"Rockrose" is the small cloth stitched in yellow, yellow-brown, and green, and has borrowed its colors and name from the plant found on the Swedish island of Öland. Of course it may also be embroidered in other colors that might better suit the surroundings in which it will be used. One may easily change the size by adding or taking away repeats. The cloth may also be sewn on coarser linen. (See page 27 for instructions for this piece.)

"August Vine," done in green leaves with the not-fully-ripe fruits of late summer, can be done in yarns of red, yellow, and brown tones, and will take on a different and more autumnlike effect. "August Vine," like most of the other designs in this book, may be sewn on coarser cloth. On the firmer D-linne, with 12 threads/cm. (30.5/in.), the embroidery may be used as a border, for example around a pillow.

# "HOLIDAY EVENING"
## (table runner)

**Pattern by:** Stig-Thore Nilsson
**Cut Size:** 25 × 95 cm. (10 × 37⅜ in.)
**Finished Size:** 18 × 84 cm. (7 × 33 in.)
**Technique:** Cross stitch
**Materials:** Irlandialinne II, 10 threads/cm. (25.5 threads/in.); HV linen yarn no. 40/2

Measure 5 cm. (2 in.) in on the short end of the linen. Begin in the middle, at the arrow. The whole table runner consists of five pattern figures. Make the hem 1 cm. (10 threads) outside the border. Notice that the colors change place in every other pattern figure.

**Yarn colors (DMC)**

HV no. 46 (310)
HV no.  9 (3021)
HV no.  8 (839)
HV no.  6 (950)

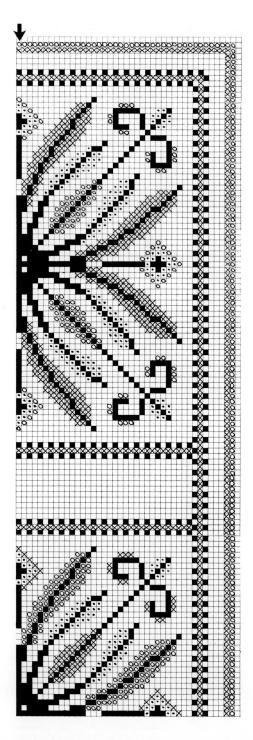

"Holiday Evening" is a stylized pattern that is repeated several times and can be very elegant as a design for the center of a large tablecloth or as a table runner, as shown here. The subtle brown colors make the embroidery look like modern wall tiles.

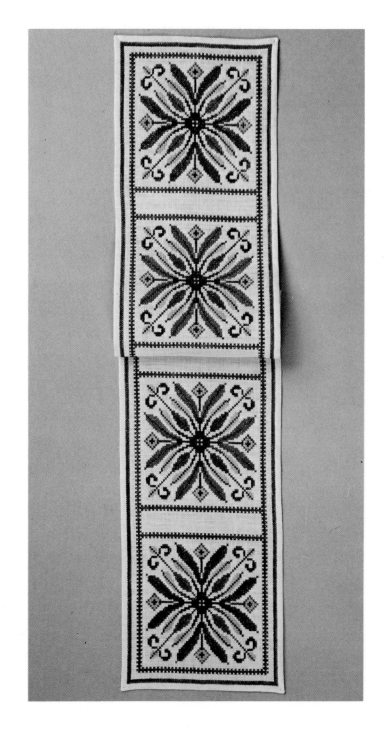

# "IN FULL BLOOM"
## (cloth)

*Pattern by:* Stig-Thore Nilsson
*Cut Size:* 35 × 35 cm. (13-3/4 × 13-3/4 in.)
*Finished Size:* 28 × 28 cm. (11 × 11 in.)
*Technique:* Cross stitch
*Materials:* D-linne, 12 threads/cm. (30.5 threads/in.); HF cotton yarn

*Yarn colors (DMC)*

| | | | |
|---|---|---|---|
| HF no. 34 (731/not good) | • • • | HF no. 504 (900) | s s s |
| HF no. 212 (3052) | ₒₒₒ | HF no. 53 (977) | T T T |
| HF no. 101 (988) | X X | HF no. 95 (921) | H H H |
| HF no. 97 (321) | V V | HF no. 48 (444) | ʌ ʌ ʌ |
| HF no. 411 (815) | /// | HF no. 206 (3051) | ▮ |
| | | HF no. 37 (956) | Ⲧ Ⲧ Ⲧ |

The flowers have been drawn in detail so that the various symbols may be seen more easily. Place them in the embroidery according to the letters and numbers.

The hem should be 12 threads wide from the outside of the cross-stitch row, and should be sewn into the cross-stitch row.

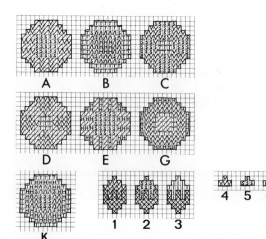

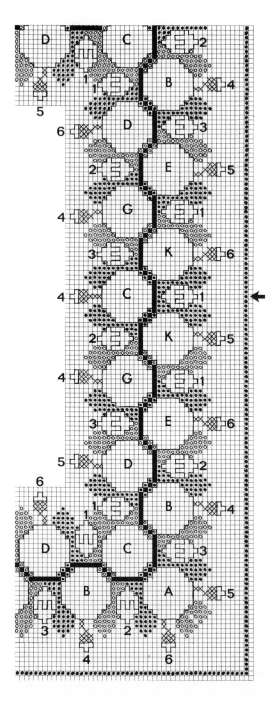

32

"In Full Bloom" was inspired by old baroque-influenced embroidery and Flemish weaving from the Swedish province of Skåne. Those who do not wish to embroider the whole cloth may use a section of it for a project such as an eyeglass case. It may also be sewn on the not so firmly woven D-linne, with 10 threads/cm. (25.5/in.).

# "CHRISTMAS ELVES' DANCE"
## (cloth)

**Pattern by:** Margareta Harström
**Cut Size:** 55 × 55 cm. (21⅔ × 21⅔ in.)
**Finished Size:** 47 × 47 cm. (18½ × 18½ in.)
**Technique:** Cross stitch
**Materials:** Dalalinne, 7.5 threads/cm. (19 threads/in.); Klippans linen yarn no. 16/2, color no. 540 (DMC: 321)

The hem is folded 11 threads outside the cross-stitch row and is hemmed into it.

# "PIGS IN PAIRS"
## (cloth)

**Pattern by:** Margareta Harström
**Cut Size:** 45 × 45 cm. (17¾ × 17¾ in.)
**Finished Size:** 39 × 39 cm. (15⅜ × 15⅜ in.)
**Technique:** Cross stitch
**Materials:** Skollinne II or Irlandialinne II, 10 threads/cm. (25.5 threads/in.); HV linen yarn no. 40/2, colors—red no. 48 (DMC: 349) or brown no. 8 (DMC: 839)

Measure 3 cm. (30 threads) in from the edge from the top and from the right side of the cloth. Begin the embroidery at the arrow. The hem is folded 6 threads outside of the last cross-stitch row and is hemmed with plain hemstitch over 2 threads inside the outer cross-stitch row. See the arrow on the pattern for the plain hemstitch.

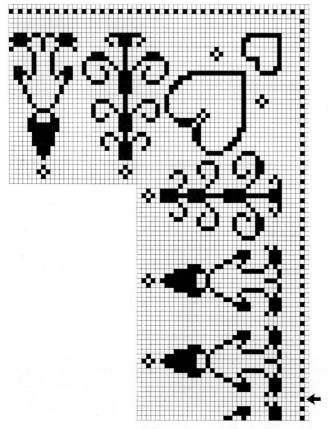

← Middle

"Christmas Elves' Dance" is a cloth that is so easily sewn that it is even suitable as children's handwork. One might want to have a red cloth for Christmas, embroidered with white or dark blue linen yarn. The pattern may also be changed to make a table runner: Place a tree alone at the short end, and embroider elves and trees along the length to the desired measurement.

"Pigs in Pairs," with a happy twist of the tail and small hearts, certainly belongs to the traditional Swedish Christmas motifs. It is not difficult to make the cloth larger or smaller so that it is suited to the table on which it will be used. With two pigs on the short side and several pairs along the length, it could be a table runner. Or, an apron for a little girl could be made with a couple of pigs on the pocket and a border on the bottom. The embroidery is also beautiful when done in brown on white.

# "SUMMER RING"
## (cloth)

*Pattern by:* Gunilla Heinemann
*Cut Size:* 70 × 70 cm. (27½ × 27½ in.)
*Finished Size:* 60 × 60 cm. (23⅔ × 23⅔ in.)
*Technique:* Cross stitch
*Materials:* Skollinne II, 10 threads/cm. (25.5 threads/in.); Klippans and Niab linen yarn no. 16/2

Measure 15 cm. (6 in.) into the fabric at the middle of one side of the linen. Begin the embroidery with the stitch shown by the arrow. The hem is folded 100 threads (10 cm. or 4 in.) from this stitch and is 10 threads wide. Hem with plain hemstitch over 2 threads.

### Yarn colors (DMC)

| PINK CLOTH | | BLUE CLOTH | |
|---|---|---|---|
| N no. 242 (3354) | ✕✕✕ | KL no. 583 (826) | ✕✕✕ |
| N no. 329 (754) | ०००  | N no. 264 (211) | ००० |
| N no. 260 (776) | ＼＼＼ | N no. 222 (3325) | ＼＼＼ |
| KL no. 625 (3348) | ▬ | N no. 206 (731) | ▬ |

"Summer Ring" is embroidered in soft colors with flower motifs that clearly derive from old samplers. The cloth may be hemmed either round or square. The small flower ring may also be repeated as the only design on a table runner, or used as a frame around initials or the year when marking household textiles.

# "UPPLAND'S GRID"
(cloth and pillow from
the Swedish province of Uppland)

## Cloth

*Pattern by:* Margareta Harström
*Cut Size:* 30 × 30 cm. (12 × 12 in.)
*Finished Size:* 22.5 × 22.5 cm. (8⅞ × 8⅞ in.)
*Technique:* Cross stitch
*Materials:* Fyenlinne, 13 threads/cm. (33 threads/in.); HF cotton yarn color no. 97 (DMC: 321)

Measure 6.5 cm. (2⅝ in.) in on the linen from above and from the left. Begin the embroidery at the arrow. The whole pattern consists of three stars on each side of the cloth and an open section in the middle (see the color plate on the facing page). A row of cross stitch is sewn 30 threads outside the pattern. The hem is folded 7 threads outside this row and is hemmed into it.

## Pillow

*Pattern by:* Margareta Harström
*Cut Size:* 37 × 75 cm. (14½ × 29½ in.)
*Finished Size:* 29 × 29 cm. (11⅜ × 11⅜ in.)
*Inside Pillow:* 30 × 30 cm. (12 × 12 in.)
*Technique:* Cross stitch
*Materials:* D-linne, 12 threads/cm. (30.5 threads/in.); HF cotton yarn, color no. 97 (DMC: 321)

Measure 7.5 cm. (3 in.) in on the linen from above and from the left. Begin the embroidery with the left-hand corner square, at the arrow. The whole pattern consists of four rows with four figures in each row. A row of cross stitch is sewn around the pattern, 12 threads outside of it.

Notice that the little square at the center of the figures, which was open on the cloth, is completely filled in on the pillow.

38

"Uppland's Grid" is a stylized pattern that is rhythmically repeated on a surface and has great usability. Here the same "star" is embroidered in different ways on the cloth and on the pillow. The motif may also be sewn on coarser linen and, of course, in other colors.

## "JOHANNA'S SAMPLER"

This is an adaptation of a sampler from the year 1828 that is part of the collection of the Nordiska Museum in Stockholm, Sweden. Johanna Åberg, from the town of Linköping, embroidered the cloth when she was thirteen years old. Originally it was sewn with silk on very fine wool and partly with cross stitch that went over only one thread. Our adaptation is 43 × 39 cm. (17 × 15⅓ in.) and is sewn with HF cotton yarn on Fyenlinne with 13 threads/cm. (33/in.).

The patterns for "Johanna's Sampler" and the wall hangings "Midsummer Dance" (page 41), "Cockatoo" (page 42), and "Clouds" (page 66) are not included in this book. Complete materials, including pattern, linen, and yarn, may be ordered from the Swedish Handcraft Society, Föreningen Svensk Hemslöjd, Sveavägen 44, 111 34 Stockholm, Sweden.

# "MIDSUMMER DANCE"
## (wall hanging)

The old traditional Swedish celebration of midsummer, centering around a flower- and foliage-decorated pole, has inspired this embroidery. Those who wish may embroider their own date and initials in the corners of the hanging. Or why not others' initials?—for certainly this hanging is an appropriate gift for a summer wedding couple. Details from the embroidery may also be used on smaller handwork. The small green border would work as a decoration on the hem of place mats or plate liners.

*Pattern by:* Stig-Thore Nilsson
*Size:* 49 × 69 cm. (19¼ × 27⅛ in.)
*Technique:* Cross stitch and backstitch
*Materials:* D-linne, 10 threads/cm. (25.5 threads/in.); HF cotton yarn

Write to the address given on page 40 for complete materials, including pattern, linen, and yarn.

# "COCKATOO"
## (wall hanging)

"Cockatoo" is a wall hanging featuring a beautiful bird in tropical lush green foliage. The cross-stitch pattern is cleverly and innovatively built up of squares and rectangles. The embroidery is neither easily nor quickly sewn if, as in the example, D-linne with 12 threads/cm. (30.5/in.) is used. However, it may also be sewn on D-linne with 10 threads/cm. (25.5/in.) or with double yarn on Dalalinne, which will make the design even larger.

*Pattern by:* Catarina Andersson
*Size:* 30.5 × 55.5 cm. (12 × 21⅞ in.)
*Technique:* Cross stitch
*Materials:* D-linne, 12 threads/cm. (30.5 threads/in.); HF cotton yarn

Write to the address given on page 40 for complete materials, including pattern, linen, and yarn.

# "DALECARLIA DELIGHT"
## (chair cushion from
## the Swedish province of Dalarna)

*Pattern by:* Karin Kessal
*Technique:* Cross stitch
*Materials:* Linneaida, 3.5 stitches/cm. (9/in.); Bergå tapestry wool. (Write to the address given on page 40 to order Bergå tapestry wool.)

### Basic pattern

Draw and cut a pattern for the chair where the cushion will be placed. Cut a sheet of foam rubber according to the pattern. The cushion should be 2.5 cm. (1 in.) thick. The basic pattern on Linneaida will be 21 cm. (8¼ in.) from the middle to the outer edge. Using this as a basis, one can increase or decrease the pattern so that it fits one's own chair. The increasing or decreasing is most easily done in the solid stripes. Begin to sew in the middle, at the arrow, so that the first leaves in the middle border are complete. Around the edge of the cushion is sewn a loose piece of cloth as high as the cushion. For the back of the cushion, use a solid-colored firm wool fabric. The cushion is then sewn together. A yarn cord in the same yarn color in which the edge is sewn, color no. 3364, is used to finish the edges, and is sewn in place by hand. Sew two pairs of ties at the back to attach the cushion to the chair.

### Yarn colors

| | | |
|---|---|---|
| B no. 3113 | B no. 3168 | B no. 3364 |
| B no. 1956 | B no. 3525 | B no. 10 |

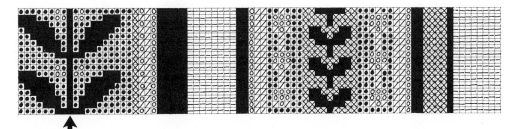

# "PEASANTRY"
## (cover for chair seat or stool)

*Pattern by:* Karin Kessal
*Technique:* Cross stitch
*Materials:* Linneaida, 3.5 stitches/cm. (9/in.); Bergå tapestry wool. (Write to the address given on page 40 to order Bergå tapestry wool.)

### Basic pattern

Refer to the "Dalecarlia Delight" chair cushion on page 43. The basic pattern may most easily be increased or decreased in the solid stripes so that the embroidery suits one's own chair or stool.

This pattern may also be used for a bench cushion if it is repeated sideways.

### Yarn Colors

| RED-GREEN CHAIR | | GRAY-BROWN CHAIR | |
|---|---|---|---|
| B no. 4258 | ⁄⁄⁄ | B no. 1533 | ⁄⁄⁄ |
| B no. 2047 | ▬ | B no. 9 | ▬ |
| B no. 4026 | ooo | B no. 1512 | ooo |
| B no. 1969 | ≡ | B no. 100 | ≡ |
| B no. 2075 | ••• | B no. 9 | ••• |
| B no. 2047 | xxx | B no. 1580 | xxx |
| B no. 3837 | \\\ | B no. 1933 | \\\ |

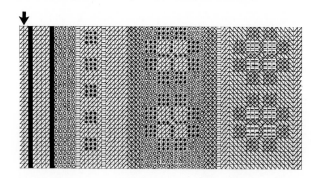

Variation of the "Peasantry" pattern

# "CHRISTENING DRESS"

Choose a simple christening-dress pattern and sew the dress in linen batiste with one whole front section and two back sections. The dress should be open in the back. Raglan sleeves are suitable (see the color plate on the facing page).

***Pattern for embroidery by:*** Stig-Thore Nilsson
***Cut Size:*** 15 × 100 cm. (6 × 39⅜ in.)
***Finished Length:*** About 91 cm. (36 in.)
***Technique:*** Cross stitch and backstitch
***Materials:*** Bleached linen 14 threads/cm. (35.5 threads/in.); HF cotton yarn; lacemaker's thread for the hem

The pattern shows the lower part of one strip. Sew thirty-nine flowers on each strip. One may either sew a scalloped edge with punch stitch (see page 67) over 3 × 3 threads, as on the model, or hem the embroidery with plain hemstitch. The hem should not be more than 6 threads wide. Before the neck edge is finished, the embroidery should be sewn on the dress. The top flower should sit 1 cm. (⅜ in.) from the edge. The embroidered strips should lie edge to edge at the top and be sewn in place so that they are 15 cm. (6 in.) apart at the hem. The neck edge is finished with an opening at the back. Sew on two white buttons and make thread loops to button into. The hem is made last.

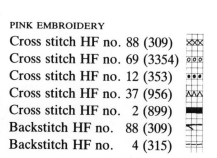

## *Yarn colors (DMC)*

| YELLOW EMBROIDERY | BLUE EMBROIDERY | PINK EMBROIDERY |
|---|---|---|
| Cross stitch HF no.   6 (831) | Cross stitch HF no.  17 (797) | Cross stitch HF no. 88 (309) |
| Cross stitch HF no. 123 (307) | Cross stitch HF no. 304   (793/not good) | Cross stitch HF no. 69 (3354) |
| Cross stitch HF no. 225 (3047) | | Cross stitch HF no. 12 (353) |
| Cross stitch HF no.  48 (444) | Cross stitch HF no.  21 (none) | Cross stitch HF no. 37 (956) |
| Cross stitch HF no.  47 (734) | Cross stitch HF no. 510 (none) | Cross stitch HF no.  2 (899) |
| Backstitch HF no.   6 (831) | Cross stitch HF no.  22 (322) | Backstitch HF no.  88 (309) |
| Backstitch HF no. 216 (3031) | Backstitch HF no.  17 (797) | Backstitch HF no.   4 (315) |
| | Backstitch HF no. 220 (336) | |

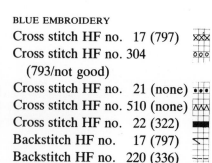

The "Christening Dress" embroidery requires many hours of work, but it will be a treasure that may be kept and used for many generations. The cross stitch is sewn on such fine linen that one may need to use an embroidery ring. Don't forget to embroider the names and dates of those who have worn the dress. If fine needlework canvas is used and basted in the thread direction, the name and date may be done in cross stitch directly on the linen batiste.

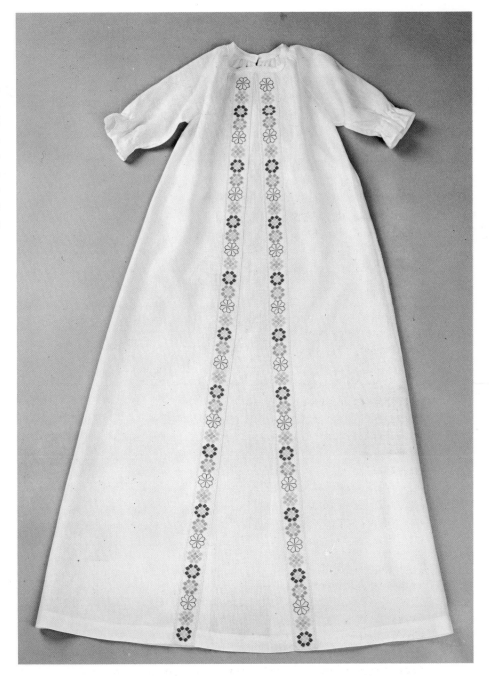

# CROSS-STITCH BORDERS

Cross-stitch borders from old samplers may be used as decorations on many articles. Here we show examples of several small cloths using these borders, which you can adapt to your own color and measurement preferences. Other suggested uses for these borders are napkin rings, closet spice bags, and so on. These small embroideries are suitable for giving as presents and are quickly sewn.

Anna I, 1818

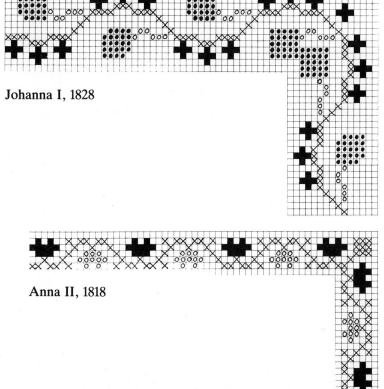

Johanna I, 1828

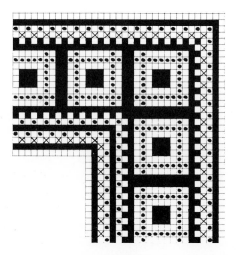

Anna II, 1818

Ingegerd, newly designed

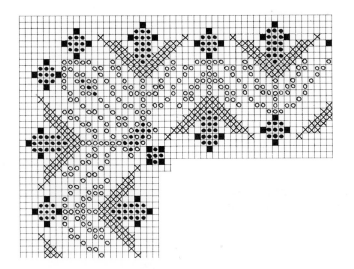

Margareta, newly designed

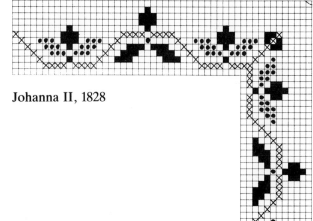

Johanna II, 1828

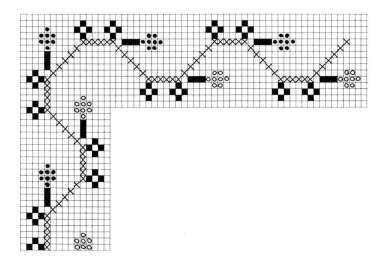

Anna III, 1818

50

# Long-legged
# Cross-Stitch Patterns

# "FOUR-LEAF CLOVER"
## (cloth)

*Pattern by:* Stig-Thore Nilsson
*Cut Size:* 43 × 43 cm. (17 × 17 in.)
*Finished Size:* 36 × 36 cm. (14⅛ × 14⅛ in.)
*Technique:* Long-legged cross stitch
*Materials:* Dalalinne, 7.5 threads/cm. (19 threads/in.); KL and Niabs linen yarn no. 16/2

All the sections marked with numbers are filled with long-legged cross stitch. The sections are sewn in the direction of the arrow according to the pattern. The hem is folded at the outermost row of long-legged cross stitch and is hemmed in the innermost (fourth) row.

*Yarn colors (DMC)*

| RED CLOTH | GREEN CLOTH |
|---|---|
| 1 = N no.  259 (600) | 1 = N no. 268 (701) |
| 2 = KL no. 634 (606) | 2 = N no. 335 (704) |
| 3 = KL no. 540 (321) | 3 = N no. 334 (702) |

| YELLOW CLOTH | BLUE CLOTH |
|---|---|
| 1 = N no.  249 (971) | 1 = N no. 270 (312) |
| 2 = KL no. 659 (972) | 2 = N no. 331 (518) |
| 3 = N no.  304 (741) | 3 = N no. 289 (826) |

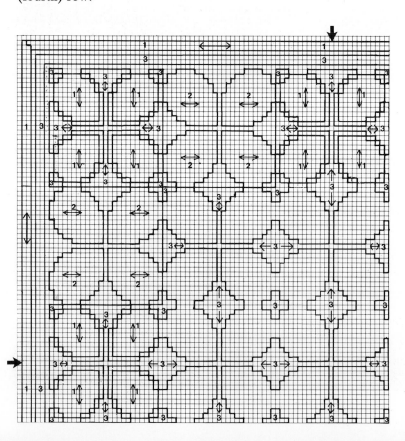

"Four-leaf Clover" is an example of a long-legged cross-stitch pattern that is a combination of filled and open clovers. In older examples of long-legged cross stitch, the embroidery usually covered the entire surface. The examples given here show embroidery in which open sections are left between the sewn pattern forms.

# PICTURES WITH FLOWER MOTIFS

### "Cornflower"

***Pattern by:*** Margareta Harström
***Cut Size:*** 25 × 30 cm. (9⅞ × 11⅞ in.)
***Finished Size:*** 18 × 22 cm. (7 × 8⅔ in.)
***Technique:*** Long-legged cross stitch
***Materials:*** Irlandialinne II, 10 threads/cm. (25.5 threads/in.); HF cotton yarn and HV linen yarn no. 40/2

All rows are sewn in a vertical direction. The embroidery is sewn with 2 threads of yarn.

***Finishing***
See page 62.

### "Ox-Eye Daisy"

***Pattern by:*** Margareta Harström
***Cut Size:*** 25 × 30 cm. (9⅞ × 11⅞ in.)
***Finished Size:*** 18 × 22 cm. (7 × 8⅔ in.)
***Technique:*** Long-legged cross stitch
***Materials:*** Irlandialinne II, 10 threads/cm. (25.5 threads/in.); HF cotton yarn and HV linen yarn no. 40/2

The embroidery is sewn with 2 threads in vertical rows, except in the white sections, which are sewn horizontally using one thread (see the graph on page 56).

***Finishing***
See page 62.

**Yarn colors for "Cornflower" (DMC)**

1 = 2 threads HF no. 203 (883)

2 = 2 threads HF no. 225 (3047)

3 = 2 threads HF no. 6 (831)

4 = 2 threads HF no. 101 (988)

5 = HF no. 8 (992/not good) + HF no. 9 (501)

6 = HF no. 224 (502) + HF no. 10 (320)

7 = 2 threads HF no. 206 (3051)

8 = HV no. 43 (3346) + HF no. 212 (3052)

9 = HF no. 0 (ecru) + HF no. 99 (368)

10 = 2 threads HV no. 33 (797)

11 = 2 threads HF no. 304 (3347/not good)

12 = 2 threads HV no. 34 (798)

13 = HV no. 33 (797) + HF no. 23 (none)

14 = 2 threads HF no. 99 (368)

15 = 2 threads HF no. 0 (ecru)

16 = 2 threads HV no. 1 (blanc)

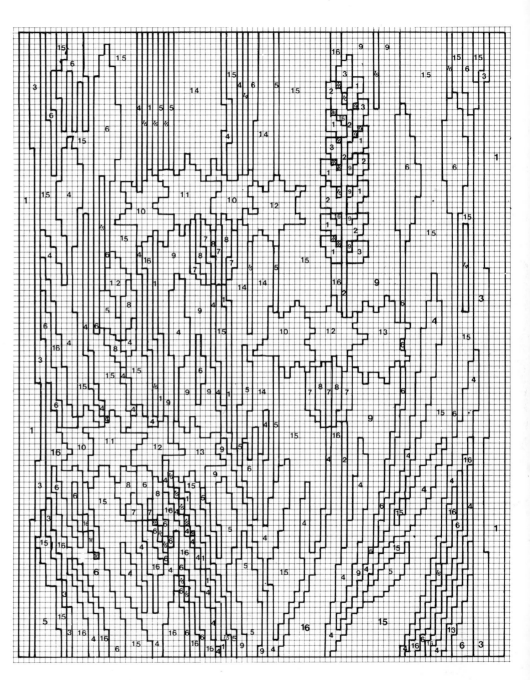

**Yarn colors for "Ox-Eye Daisy" (DMC)**

1 = 2 threads HF no. 220
(336)

2 = 2 threads HF no. 228
(none)

3 = 2 threads HV no. 45 (791/
not good)

4 = 2 threads HV no. 34 (798)

5 = 2 threads HF no. 22 (322)

6 = 2 threads HV no. 38 (518)

7 = 1 thread HF no. 0 (ecru)

8 = 2 threads HF no. 508
(911)

9 = 2 threads HV no. 40 (991)

10 = HF no. 40 (989) + HF
no. 505 (704)

11 = 2 threads HF no. 506
(3347/not good)

12 = 2 threads HF no. 9 (501)

13 = 2 threads HF no. 210
(500)

14 = 2 threads HV no. 44 (725)

15 = 1 thread HV no. 1 (blanc)

16 = 2 threads HF no. 507
(702)

17 = HF no. 100 (367) + HF
no. 101 (988)

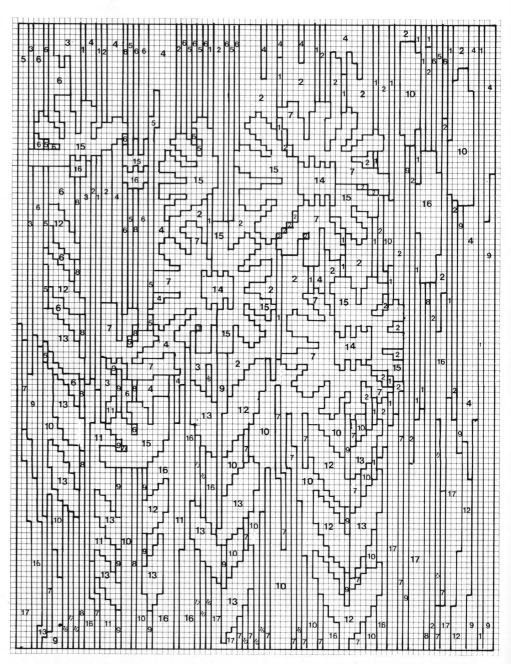

56

## "Twin Flower"
### ("Linnea," after the Swedish botanist Carolus Linnaeus)

*Pattern by:* Margareta Harström
*Cut Size:* 25 × 30 cm. (9⅞ × 11⅞ in.)
*Finished Size:* 18 × 22 cm. (7 × 8⅔ in.)
*Technique:* Long-legged cross stitch
*Materials:* Irlandialinne II, 10 threads/cm. (25.5 threads/in.); HF cotton yarn and HV linen yarn no. 40/2

The embroidery is sewn with 2 threads of yarn. All rows are sewn in a vertical direction in the X-marked sections; sew every other row with 2 threads of HF no. 34 (DMC: 731). (See graph on page 58.)

*Finishing*
See page 62.

## "Checkered Daffodil"

*Pattern by:* Margareta Harström
*Cut Size:* 25 × 30 cm. (9⅞ × 11⅞ in.)
*Finished Size:* 18 × 22 cm. (7 × 8⅔ in.)
*Technique:* Long-legged cross stitch
*Materials:* Irlandialinne II, 10 threads/cm. (25.5 threads/in.); HF cotton yarn and HV linen yarn no. 40/2

The embroidery is sewn with 2 threads of the yarn. All rows are sewn in a vertical direction. (See graph on page 59.)

*Finishing*
See page 62.

*Yarn colors for "Twin Flower" (DMC)*

1 = HF no. 9 (501) + HF no. 100 (367)

2 = HF no. 34 (731/not good) + HF no. 212 (3052)

3 = HF no. 506 (3347/not good) + HF no. 507 (702)

4 = 2 threads HF no. 212 (3052)

5 = HF no. 302 (3053) + HF no. 224 (502)

6 = HF no. 7 (644) + HF no. 223 (none)

7 = 2 threads HV no. 1 (blanc)

8 = 2 threads HF no. 0 (ecru)

9 = 2 threads HF no. 2 (899)

10 = 2 threads HF no. 69 (3354)

11 = HF no. 69 (3354) + HV no. 23 (353)

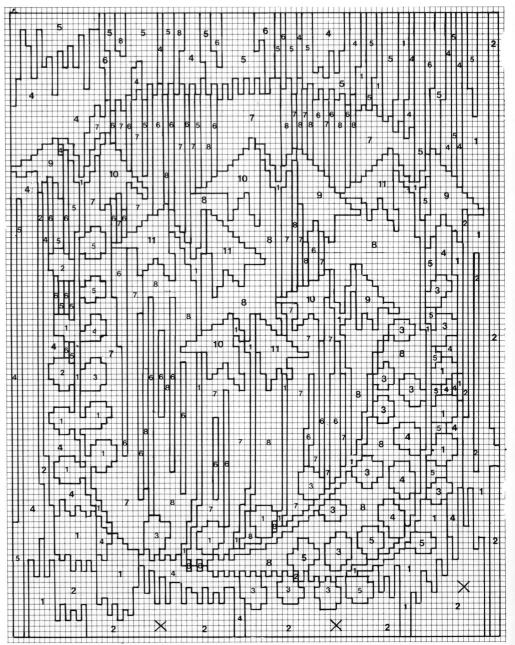

 1 = 2 threads HF no. 69
(3354)

 2 = 2 threads HF no. 2 (899)

 3 = 2 threads HF no. 323
(223)

 4 = 2 threads HF no. 0 (ecru)

 5 = HF no. 0 (ecru) + HF
no. 303 (415)

 6 = HF no. 303 (415) + HF
no. 7 (644)

 7 = 2 threads HF no. 34 (731/
not good)

 8 = 2 threads HF no. 223
(none)

 9 = HV no. 43 (3346) + HF
no. 212 (3052)

10 = HF no. 302 (3053) + HF
no. 99 (368)

11 = 2 threads HF no. 215
(640)

12 = 2 threads HV no. 8 (839)

## "Wild Pansy"

**Pattern by:** Margareta Harström
**Cut Size:** 25 × 30 cm. (9⅞ × 11⅞ in.)
**Finished Size:** 18 × 22 cm. (7 × 8⅔ in.)
**Technique:** Long-legged cross stitch
**Materials:** Irlandialinne II, 10 threads/cm. (25.5 threads/in.); HF cotton yarn and HV linen yarn no. 40/2

The embroidery is sewn with 2 threads of the yarn. All of the rows, except those with arrows on the pattern, are sewn in a vertical direction. Those with arrows are sewn in a horizontal direction. In the large X-marked sections, it is suitable to sew some rows in the middle of the section with 2 threads of the darker color in order to achieve color variation. (See graph on page 61.)

**Finishing**
See page 62.

## "Water Lily"

**Pattern by:** Margareta Harström
**Cut Size:** 25 × 30 cm. (9⅞ × 11⅞ in.)
**Finished Size:** 18 × 22 cm. (7 × 8⅔ in.)
**Technique:** Long-legged cross stitch
**Materials:** Irlandialinne II, 10 threads/cm. (25.5 threads/in.); HF cotton yarn and HV linen yarn no. 40/2

The embroidery is sewn with 2 threads of the yarn. All rows are sewn in a vertical direction. (See graph on page 62.)

**Yarn colors for "Wild Pansy" (DMC)**

1 = 2 threads HV no. 19 (741)

2 = 1 thread HF no. 0 (ecru)

3 = HV no. 32 (none) + HF no. 11 (3041/not good)

4 = HV no. 28 (327/not good) + HF no. 11 (3041/not good)

5 = 2 threads HF no. 232 (554/not good)

6 = 2 threads HF no. 302 (3053)

7 = HF no. 9 (501) + HF no. 10 (320)

8 = HF no. 100 (367) + HF no. 101 (988)

9 = HF no. 100 (367) + HF no. 210 (500)

10 = 2 threads HF no. 210 (500)

11 = HF no. 220 (336) + HF no. 147 (none)

12 = HF no. 216 (3031) + HF no. 210 (500)

13 = 1 thread HV no. 1 (blanc)

## Yarn colors for "Water Lily" (DMC)

1 = 2 threads HF no. 210 (500)

2 = 2 threads HF no. 9 (501)

3 = HF no. 226 (none) + HF no. 211 (991)

4 = HF no. 8 (992/not good) + HF no. 100 (367)

5 = 2 threads HF no. 212 (3052)

6 = 2 threads HF no. 223 (none)

7 = HF no. 99 (368) + HF no. 223 (none)

8 = 2 threads HV no. 1 (blanc)

9 = HF no. 0 (ecru) + HF no. 99 (368)

10 = 2 threads HF no. 0 (ecru)

11 = 2 threads HF no. 53 (977)

### Finishing

Sew a row of stem stitch around the entire embroidery. Sew with 2 threads and choose the color that is used the most near the edge. Then fold the hem tightly at the edge of the embroidery and hem on the back side.

As has been done with "Water Lily," the pictures may be mounted on a firm linen-covered backing in a suitable color, or they may be stretched in a frame. Two, three, or more of these flower motifs may also be embroidered in a row for a beautiful wall hanging.

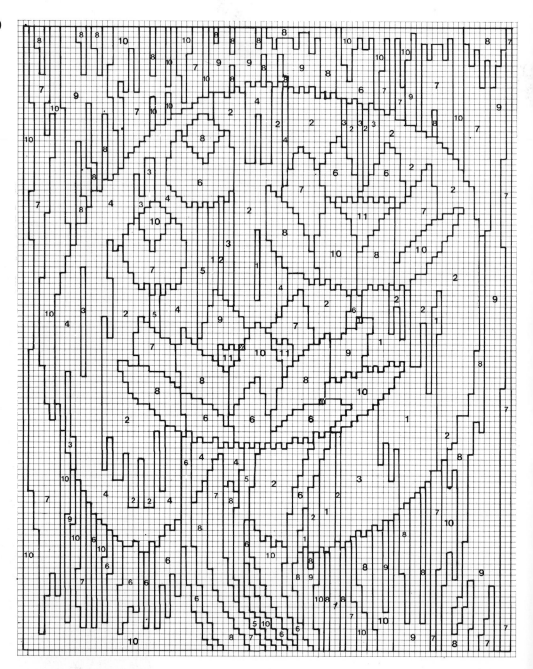

# "MADAM"
## (handbag)

As in the "Four-leaf Clover" cloth, only the pattern on this handbag has been embroidered and the background has been left unfilled. The pattern has fewer sections of embroidery at the top and more at the bottom. This places the weight of the pattern at the lower part of the handbag.

**Pattern by:** Margareta Harström
**Cut Size, Front:** 43 × 45 cm. (17 × 17¾ in.)
**Finished Size:** 33 × 35.5 cm. (13 × 14 in.)
**Cut Size, Back:** 42 × 40 cm. (16½ × 15¾ in.)
**Cut Size, Lining:** 80 × 40 cm. (31½ × 15¾ in.)
**Technique:** Long-legged cross stitch
**Materials:** Dalalinne, 7.5 threads/cm. (19 threads/ in.) for the front; wool fabric for the back; taffeta or cotton fabric for the lining; KL and Niabs linen yarn no. 16/2

Measure 3 cm. (22 threads) in from the right and from the top of the linen. Begin the embroidery at the bold arrow on the pattern. Those sections marked with arrows are sewn with rows in the direction of the arrows. All other sections are sewn horizontally.

The example is sewn with two-row long-legged cross stitch.

### Yarn colors (DMC)

BLACK
1 = KL no. 599 (310)
2 = KL no. 516 (535)
3 = KL no. 512 (452)
4 = N no.   220 (762)

RED
1 = KL no. 635 (355)
2 = N no.   229 (3328)
3 = KL no. 535 (351)
4 = KL no. 633 (761)

GREEN
1 = N no.   314 (500)
2 = N no.   235 (501)
3 = N no.   311 (966)
4 = KL no. 519 (503)

### Finishing

Sew together the front and back sections of the handbag on the wrong side. Leave the sides open 7 to 8 cm. (3 in.) from the top of the pattern. Press open the seams. Then sew a casing at the top on both the front and back sides. Sew together a lining fabric in a suitable color (leave this open 3 inches from the top also). Place the lining in the handbag with the seams together and slip-stitch the two fabrics together at the top edge and down the openings. Buy handles with thin metal rods at the bottom and thread them into the casings.

# "CLOUDS"
## (wall hanging)

The designer of this piece must have been looking into space when she composed it—a condensation of innumerable stars in blue and white. The background is richly varied; the many yellow nuances have been achieved by the mixing of two or three threads of different colors.

*Pattern by:* Margareta Harström
*Size:* 43 × 75.5 cm. (17 × 29¾ in.)
*Technique:* Long-legged cross stitch
*Materials:* Dalalinne, 7.5 threads/cm. (19 threads/in.); linen yarn 16/2, 1 thread; cotton yarn 24/2, 3 threads; linen yarn 40/2, 3 threads

See page 40 for the address to write to for complete materials, including pattern, linen, and yarn.

66

# Finishing

## PUNCH-STITCH EDGE

A punch-stitch edge is sewn in the following manner. First, sew a row of backstitch in the edge where the hem will be folded (Figure 1). All the stitches should be firmly drawn (the diagram does not show this). Next, fold the hem and sew punch stitch through the double thickness. Punch stitch begins with two horizontal stitches (Figures 2 and 3). The third stitch is sewn vertically (Figure 4). Then the stitches are repeated from Figure 1. When the first row is sewn around the cloth, a second row is sewn where all the stitches are taken double except for the outermost stitch; see the striped stitches in Figure 5. Taking double stitches causes the holes to be more easily seen. Finally, trim off the extra fabric on the back of the cloth.

Figure 6 shows a finished punch-stitch edge.

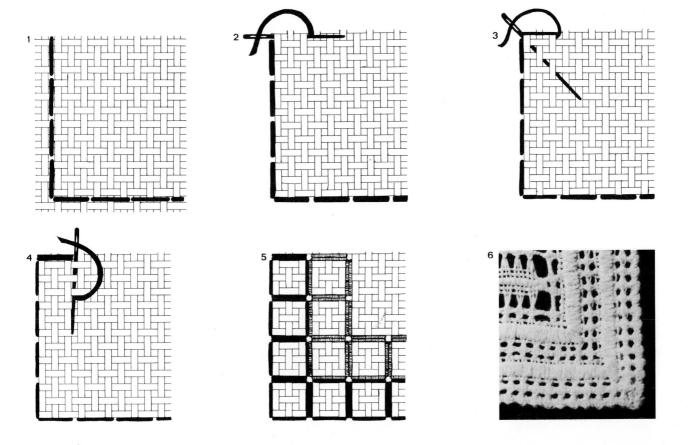

# HEMSTITCH HEM

A hemstitch hem is usually sewn over three threads. However, it may also be sewn over 2 threads, or 4 or more, depending on the firmness of the linen. Hemstitch may, according to the different patterns, have different names, such as plain or double hemstitch, but it is always sewn in the same manner. The striped section of the diagram below (Figure 1) shows the folded hem from the back side. First, sew one stitch over 3 threads and then take a little stitch in the hem, and so forth. The stitch in the hem should not be seen from the right side.

Figure 2 shows a finished hemstitch hem.

# MITERED CORNERS

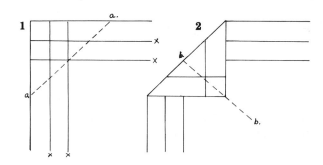

Following a thread of the fabric, first make the folds for double hems around the entire work (X on Figure 1), so that the folds can easily be seen when the linen is smoothed flat again. Then make a fold to the wrong side, according to the dotted line (*a* on Figure 1). Make a fold to the right side, according to the dotted line (*b* in Figure 2). Sew together (*c* in Figure 3) with fine overhand stitches. Pull out the fold and cut away the unnecessary fabric, according to the dotted line (*d* in Figure 4). Press open the seam, turn the corner, and hem.

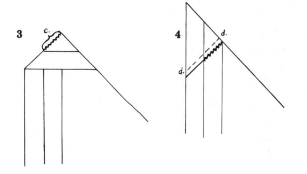

# STRAIGHT CORNERS

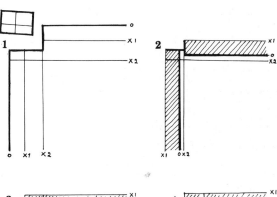

Straight corners are easier to do than mitered corners. They are used for small hems in open weaves or in instances where the hems are of different widths. First fold straight, following a thread of the fabric, the folds for double hems around the entire work (X1 and X2 on Figure 1), so that the folds can easily be seen when the linen is smoothed flat again. The line marked 0 is the cut edge of the linen. Cut out the corner as shown in Figure 1. The first fold is made on both sides of the corner (Figure 2). Then fold the side where the most has been cut away (Figure 3). Finally, fold the other side, as shown in Figure 4, and hem.

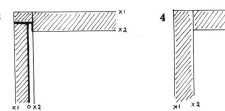

# Stitching Aids

The experienced embroiderer's skill is acquired by long hours of training of hand and eye. But many of the disappointments that beginners suffer can be avoided if one uses the aids that are available. The stitches lie much better if the fabric is stretched during work. For large work, use of a sewing frame (see diagram) is preferable, and for smaller work an embroidery ring. Both are available in various sizes. Don't forget when you use an embroidery ring to wind thin cotton bands around the ring, so the fabric will not glide during the work. If it is difficult to see and count on fine linen, one may use a sewing glass. Different types of sewing glasses are available, but the simplest is a magnifying glass worn on a string around the neck and supported against the chest. Finally, it is important that one does not use too thick a needle. There must not be a larger hole in the fabric than the yarn can fill.

## STRETCHING FABRIC IN A SEWING FRAME

The sewing frame consists of eight parts (see diagram): two strong ribs (a) with cloth bands nailed onto them (c) and holes for the two smaller ribs (b), which have several holes bored for the four pegs (d).

Sew the short sides of the embroidery fabric to the cloth band (c), following a straight thread of the fabric. Then place the small ribs (b) in the holes provided in the larger ribs (a). Place the pegs in the proper holes along the small ribs (b) so that the fabric is adequately stretched. With strong thread, sew alternately into the embroidery fabric and around the rib (b).

The frame is supported against a table while the embroidery work is done with the right hand over and the left hand under the fabric.

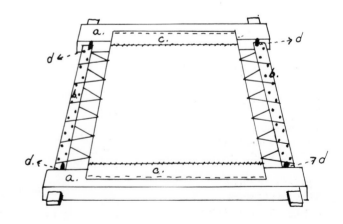

# Suppliers

Haandarbejdets Fremmes cotton yarn may be purchased from the firm's general agent in the United States: Ginnie Thompson Originals, P.O. Box 930, Pawley's Island, S.C. 29585 (toll-free number, 800-845-8073). Or contact one of the following shops:

Algerian Eye, Inc.
2108 Brandon Street, S.W.
Huntsville, Ala. 35801

The Needlework Shop (Inc.)
21 B Peninsula Center
Rolling Hills, Calif. 90274

The Friend Ship
465 East Green Street
Pasadena, Calif. 91101

Stitchcraft Store
3928 Clairmont Mesa Boulevard
San Diego, Calif. 92117

The Status Thimble
311 Primrose Road
Burlingame, Calif. 94070

Thumbelina
1688 Copenhagen Drive
Solvang, Calif. 93463

Carolea's "Knitche"
586 South Murphy
Sunnyvale, Calif. 94086

Fiesta Yarn Shop
5752 Wadsworth Boulevard
Arvada, Colo. 80002

The Needleworker
314 Columbine Street
Denver, Colo. 80206

The Needlecrafter, Ltd.
2081 30th Street
Boulder, Colo. 80301

Yarn Crafts
125 North College
Fort Collins, Colo. 80524

The Giving Tree
248 Giralda Avenue
Coral Gables, Fla. 33134

Elite Design
P.O. Box 894
503 South Thornton Avenue
Dalton, Ga. 30720

Stitchcraft Studio
495 Main
Boise, Idaho 83702

The Little Needlepoint Shop
830 State
Bettendorf, Iowa 52722

The Stitching Post
2354 Front Street
Slidell, La. 70458

Cross Stitch Corner
4001-A Lakeshore Drive
Shreveport, La. 71109

The Needlecraft Shop
68 Cranbrook Road
Cockeysville, Md. 21030

Town-Ho Antiques and Needlework
1912 Main Street
Brewster, Mass. 02631

Spinning Wheel, Inc.
10 South 15th Avenue E
Duluth, Minn. 55812

The Needlework Shop
Royal Ridge Mall
Nashua, N.H. 03060

The Yarn Loft, Inc.
50 State Street
Pittsford, N.Y. 14534

Eager Weavers
182 Jefferson Road
Rochester, N.Y. 14623

The Scotch Bonnet Needle Arts Studio, Inc.
1309 West 14th Street
Greenville, N.C. 27834

The Balcony
104 Orange Street
Wilmington, N.C. 28401

Creative Needles
2221 North Center
Hickory, N.C. 28601

Nimble Needle
10700 Mayfield Road
Chardon, Ohio 44024

The Daisy Barrel
510 West Xenia Drive
Fairborn, Ohio 45324

Threads N' Things
109 Whitehall Road
Anderson, S.C. 29621

The Counting House
P.O. Box 155
Pawley's Island, S.C. 29585

The Canvas Corner
2822 Rennoc Road
Knoxville, Tenn. 37918

Julie's Needle Art Shop
111 Racine
Memphis, Tenn. 38111

Needle In A Haystack
6911 Preston Road
Dallas, Tex. 75205

Needlework Patio
6925 Snider Plaza
Dallas, Tex. 75205

The Needle Art Shop
16540 El Camino Road
Houston, Tex. 77062

Persian Yarn Connection
4208 Arbordale West
Tacoma, Wash. 98466

Needle Art Studio
17700 West Capitol Drive
Brookfield, Wis. 53005

Fibre Arts
6606 West North Avenue
Wauwatosa, Wis. 53213

Witchery Stitchery
132 East Main Street
Mt. Horeb, Wis. 53572

HF cotton yarn is sold in Great Britain as Danish Flower Threads and is available from the following suppliers:

The Silver Thimble
33 Gay Street
Bath
Avon BA1 2NT

Leven Crafts
The Minstrels Gallery
21 Chaloner Street
Guisborough
Cleveland

The Campden Needlecraft Centre
High Street
Chipping Campden
Gloucestershire

Ladies Work Society Ltd.
Delabere House
New Road
Moreton-in-Marsh
Gloucestershire GL56 OAS

Brodwaith Embroidery
5 Lion Yard
Dolgellau
Gwynedd
Wales

Christine Riley
53 Barclay Street
Stonehaven
Kincardineshire AB3 2AR
Scotland

The Danish Shop
16 Sloane Street
London SWIX 9NB

The Danish Embroidery Centre Ltd.
The Old Rectory
Claydon
Ipswich
Suffolk IP6 OEQ

The Spinning Jenny
Bradley
Keighley
West Yorkshire BD20 9DD

Mace & Nairn
89 Crane Street
Salisbury
Wiltshire SP1 2PY

De Denne Limited
159/161 Kenton Road
Kenton
Harrow
Middlesex